Making
Electricity

Focus: Systems
Materials

PETER SLOAN &
SHERYL SLOAN

This is a power station.
This power station uses
water to make electricity.

2

The power station has large
motors, called turbines.
Water drives the turbines.
Turbines use this power
to drive machines called
generators.

This is a large generator.
The generator has big
magnets inside wire loops.
As the generator spins
around it makes electricity.

The electricity from the generator is fed into electric wires. The electric wires carry the power to substations. The substations are near where people live.

Wires carry the electricity
from the substation to
the houses. The wires are
connected to the house
at the meter. The meter
shows how much power
has been used.

In the house, wires carry
the electricity to the lights
and plugs in the rooms.
The wires are covered to
protect them and stop
them from causing sparks.
The wires are built into the
walls of the house.

The television, toaster, or
hair dryer cord is put into
the plug. It can be turned
on or off with the flick of
a switch. The electricity
has come a long way
to make these electrical
machines work.